WHAT IS A FOSSIL?

First Steck-Vaughn Edition 1992

Copyright © 1989 American Teacher Publications

Published by Steck-Vaughn Company

Library of Congress number: 89-3559

Library of Congress Cataloging in Publication Data.

Goldish, Meish.
  What is a fossil?

  (Real readers)
  Summary: Examines different kinds of fossils, how they are formed, and what they say about the world.
  1. Paleontology—Juvenile literature. [1. Fossils. 2. Paleontology] I. Dieruf, Ivan, ill. Title. III. Series.
  QE714.5.G65 1989   560   89-3559

ISBN 0-8172-3535-3   hardcover library binding

ISBN 0-8114-6734-1   softcover binding

    6 7 8 9 0   96

WHAT IS A

FOSSIL?

by Meish Goldish
illustrated by Ivan Dieruf

RSVP
RAINTREE
STECK-VAUGHN
PUBLISHERS
The Steck-Vaughn Company

Austin, Texas

There was a time when there were many dinosaurs in the world.

There are no dinosaurs now. But we do know that dinosaurs lived very long ago. We know this because people have found dinosaur bones and other fossils.

What is a fossil? A fossil is part or all of an animal or a plant that lived very long ago. Dinosaur bones are just one kind of fossil.

How did something that was once alive become a fossil?

Some fossils were made in mud. Here is how one dinosaur became a fossil in mud.

The dinosaur swam in a lake 190 million years ago. When the dinosaur died, it sank into the mud at the bottom of the lake.

Mud covered the dinosaur. The dinosaur began to rot. After a while, only its bones were left. The bones lay in the mud for millions of years.

As more time passed, the mud around the dinosaur bones turned into rock. The bones became as hard as rock, too. What was once a dinosaur is now a fossil.

Today, the lake is dry. The bottom of the lake is a stone bed. If people dig in the stone bed, they might find the dinosaur bones. They will find a fossil of a very old dinosaur!

Sometimes a fossil is a print of something that lived long ago.

When you walk in mud, your feet make prints. About 100 million years ago, a dinosaur walked in mud. As time passed, the mud got hard. The mud turned to stone. People have found fossil prints of dinosaur feet. The prints are very, very big and very, very old!

About 300 million years ago, a leaf fell from a tree. It landed in sand. The sand turned very hard over the years. The leaf rotted away. But it left a print in the sand. A print of a leaf is another kind of fossil.

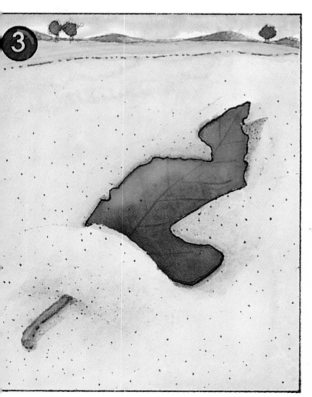

Not all fossils are found in rock. Some are found in sap. Sap is yellow and sticky. It drips out of some trees.

An ant was on a tree 250 million years ago. It got stuck in the sap. The sap ran all over the ant. In time, the sap turned hard. It looked like yellow glass. The ant did not rot in the sap. Today, the ant looks the same as it did long ago.

An animal stuck in hard, yellow sap is another kind of fossil.

A fossil may be found in tar, too. Fossils of big cats called saber-toothed tigers have been found in tar pits in California. These animals lived more than 40 thousand years ago.

Once, an animal that looked like an elephant was found in ice in Siberia. The animal that was found is called a woolly mammoth, and it lived about 20 thousand years ago. It was eating grass when it died. The grass was still in its mouth!

Scientists can use fossils to find out what the world was like millions of years ago.

People have found fossils of sea shells in the cliffs of the Grand Canyon. Today, the Grand Canyon is very far from the sea. The fossils help scientists to know that once the Grand Canyon was under the sea.

People have found fossils from palm trees in Scotland. Scotland is cold. Palm trees can only grow in hot places. The fossils help scientists know that once Scotland was a hot place.

Scientists have found fossils of dinosaur eggs, too! Inside these eggs were baby dinosaurs called hadrosaurs. These eggs help scientists to know that the baby hadrosaurs came from eggs, just the way baby chicks do today.

Where can you find fossils? Fossils can be found in many places.

Look at the beach or by a river. Look in a park or in the woods. Look in the big stone walls you see in the city. Maybe you will find a fossil!

Sharing the Joy of Reading

Beginning readers enjoy reading books on their own. Reading a book is a worthwhile activity in and of itself for a young reader. However, a child's reading can be even more rewarding if it is shared. This sharing can enhance your child's appreciation— both of the book and of his or her own abilities.

Now that your child has read **What Is a Fossil?**, you can help extend your child's reading experience by encouraging him or her to:

- Retell the story or key concepts presented in this story in his or her own words. The retelling can be oral or written.

- Create a picture of a favorite character, event, or concept from this book.

- Express his or her own ideas and feelings about the subject of this book and other things he or she might want to know about this subject.

Here is an activity that you can do together to help extend your child's appreciation of this book: You and your child can make a fossil-like print together. Use modeling clay, or else make clay dough. To make clay dough, you will need 1 cup flour, $\frac{1}{4}$ cup salt, and $\frac{1}{3}$ cup water. Mix the flour with the salt. Then mix in enough water to make a stiff dough, about the consistency of pie dough. Shape the dough into a ball and cover with plastic wrap. Let stand for 15 minutes. Now you have ready-to-use clay dough.

When the clay is ready, shape it into a flat, rectangular slab, large enough for your child's hand to rest on. Then have your child place his or her hand on the slab and press down. When the hand is lifted, a print will be left in the clay. If you use the clay dough, the print can be dried or baked in the oven, then painted.